Provincetown
poems and paintings

Joan Cofrancesco
Illustrations by Janine Bartolotti

AuthorHouse™
1663 Liberty Drive
Bloomington, IN 47403
www.authorhouse.com
Phone: 1 (800) 839-8640

Published by AuthorHouse 05/13/2016

ISBN: 978-1-5246-0900-9 (sc)
ISBN: 978-1-5246-0901-6 (e)

authorHOUSE®

joan cofrancesco and janine bartolotti have been vacationing in provincetown for years. the city has inspired joan's poetry and and janine's watercolors.

syracuse is a blues town
from the festivals
to the dinosaur
let's go to soho
or greece
or some leather bar
in provincetown
and then to the horses
at santa anita

i have to
get this
20 pound
black cat
off my chest
and get us packed
for provincetown

p-town

low tide
we walked out
to the lighthouse
and slowly
became engulfed

provincetown morning

red boats
are leaning on their sides
seagulls are blue
dunes are purple
a young hot dyke
walks by
with a white dog

pizza crusts
on paper plates
empty beer cans

lava lamp casts
blue green
shadow on the wall

black cat
beside me

on hardwood floor

it was all an illusion—
all of your lofty things
the woodfire
dreams
zen
the cat
paris
six a.m.
e=mc2
the dunes of cape cod
your love for me

i saw the moon
in my wine glass
and i thought of
li po

on the beach
she was reading
colin wilson
i had to talk to her
i'm still talking to her

provincetown:
rainbow colored umbrellas
raised against
the bright sun

fall asleep
in a hammock
under the sun
wake up
under stars

turn water into wine
walk across the ocean,
rise from the dead,
all in a days
poem

lately my dreams
are cats
basking
in
the
sun

haiku

at provincetown beach
a man in shorts takes photos
of naked bathers

after cavafy
affair with a married woman

above a gay bar in provincetown
the bed had satin sheets
the musk of her coming
and coming
her huge breasts
rising and pressing
against my mouth
those thursday afternoons
even years later

naked young
portuguese woman
lying
in the black sand
bright yellow sun
between her thighs

race point

drinking wine
reading frank o'hara
shamelessly
on the beach

the ocean is shining
like a sapphire
i sit in a noisy outdoor café
sipping merlot
reading hacker
as the waiter
serves me the head
of john the baptist
on a gold platter

lips wet
with sex
our bodies sizzle
in the sun

rolling waves
hit the sand
no thoughts of tomorrow

i'd drink
expensive red
with my toast every morning
i'd look like angelina
and write like frank
i'd live in provincetown
in a loft overlooking the sea
with 10 siamese cats
who all have blue
crossed eyes

i believe

i fast
i drink no wine
i sleep alone
i dream
i walk
on the ocean
until 1000 waves
curl around me
and
pull me under

2 women
intertwined
on a mattress
on the floor
candles
incense
wind chimes

provincetown
    (to ted berrigan)

beautiful lesbians
purple candles
hand asleep
nothing happened

three days
incense
candles
writing
balling
pizza boxes
cat sitting
with its back to us

after
noon
sex

casablanca fan
cools the sweat
on our backs

race point

tourists zoom
their lenses
at the sunset—
6 seals catch my eye

in my dream
you were turning
water to wine
and multiplying
fish and loaves
and i was stealing away
with your sandals
on black sand

poem after schuler

my muse lifts weights
and has a body like
martina navratilova
my muse wears gucci
sunglasses
and looks great in them
i could go on
and
on
and
on

THE MOORS

after sappho

some say
it's the sunset
over provincetown
or santorini
i say
it's whatever
you love
i say
it's you

cape cod

i feel the smoothness
of your thighs
beneath mine
the breeze from the window
smells of the sea
on the undrunk bottle of dry
red wine

it's normal

i love to sleep
in a cottage
in provincetown
and
hear the rain
pounding the roof
and the gay
guys next
door
banging
away
to
club
music
and then
waking up
with
you and
collect
shells
and
stones
along
the beach

RACE POINT

the spirited
young men
outside
spiritus pizza
provincetown
the smell of
expensive colognes
mixed with sweat
everybody
leaves the bars
to get a slice
and a coke

fisherman's wharf
p-town t-shirts
suntan lotion
sunglasses
whale watch boats
2 lesbians
holding hands

rolling waves
hit the sand
sooth the pain
in our oz-like existence
we have
no thoughts
of tomorrow

still-life with cats

sitting here on my futon
drinking another bottle of rum
i've been thinking about you
all the times we drove out
from syracuse to provincetown
a bottle between us

when we got there
we made slow love to each other
in a cold bed
by the ocean
always staying at the same place
6 blue cats
in the yard

provincetown cats

inside the warm inn
a thin braided rug
domesticates the guest room, huge cats
everywhere
inhabit the couch, and when there's
a strong wind warning, we get the
fire going
read melville's
moby dick, or
sit looking out at the waves, as they curl
and tuck themselves under like
the cats in the guest room
at the ship's bell inn

night ocean

we ride the full moon atlantic
the water cold and turbulent
stars guide us
whales jump everywhere
minke whales are breaching
i hand you a hot chocolate with marshmallows
to warm you
our souls move in and out of
ourselves like lovers
once again we challenge fate
straddle the blade
that we both realize
is there

we slept together for six years
under satin sheets

in that cottage by the sea
our books
our collection of bones
laid out on cotton
like gold
& our 5 round orange cats
running around in moonlight

now mail piles in corners
and there's dust everywhere

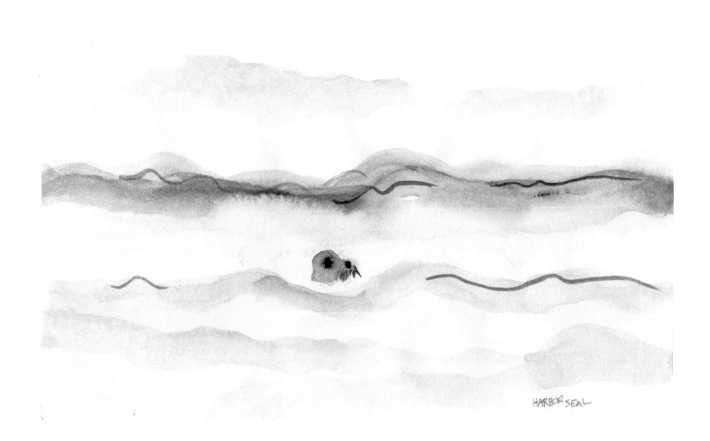

HARBOR SEAL

55

provincetown gym

he wore a tomcat t-shirt
as he prowled around the gym
there was something about him
that i liked
his nike sneakers and perfect
butt
his tight black shorts
the way he would strut
over to the weights
like a muscular black panther

another 4am poem

i set the alarm at 4am
to drive to
provincetown

cats walk the slats
of the city morning
in summer
fight on the fire-escape
i disregard them
but pack my nike sneakers,
beach ball, cosmic mama's magic
brownies, maps

the light comes
into my window
wavering over my world
of blues,
jazz, and old photos

i can hear someone
else's tv
as i pack my car

soon i will be there—
washing the city sounds
into the ocean.

poet in a dunescape

it began with sand,
then came the clamshell path,
the lobster-traps, with seaweed around them,
the leaky-drinking trough under the acadia tree
where giraffes used to stand
amidst rippled grasses

then came night
that was like dripping water.
at times, for days
a spirit flew,
half bird, half horse
just above the straw roof
from where a coyote howled.

it was there
she forgot about death
on the tattered rice paper
the flickering candlelight in the window.

the poem that i will be remembered for

my best poem will have ocean
right in the middle of it, ocean so cold and deep
with life my friend will leave behind
his scuba outfit and tell me, "wear this when you
go in." my best poem
will have night in it, too, and all the stars
in the eastern sky; and this immense body
of water shining for miles under a full moon.
my best poem will have a jacuzzi
and a shower for itself, skylights,
a phone by the faucet,
a soapdish made from a clam shell
picked from the beach an hour before breakfast.
there'll be waves breaking in my best poem;
and a beach where ocean-soaked
shellfish will rise up, consuming one another.
oh, my best poem will throw tides!
but there won't be any waterglasses in my best poems
i'll take up drinking from the bottle.

watching the sunset
over race point beach with you
and merlot
your feet on my lap

condoms on the sand
between the seaweed and shells
drag queens
on tricycles
i dive naked
into the ocean

coming into p-town
identical wooden cottages
all in a row
now that's understatement

black dog
running on sand
against blue ocean
nobody owns me

backpack for p-town
bob marley
and some joints

there would have been
a poem here
but my dog ate it

in the shadows of the bar
high black beehive hairdo
of the queen

strolling
hand in hand
along the beach
which part of the sand castle
is left?

early morning walk
along race point
a painter
rides his canvas chair
into the blue

normal here
a drag queen
in the hardware store
buying nails

did the starfish
fall out of the sky?

nothing like
the leftovers
at nappys
for cape cod cats

sleeping in the
shaggy cape dunes—
flying seagulls

for inspiration
wine walk wind
and waves

race point beach
harbor seals raise their heads
or are they dogs

panties left on sand
what happened last night
by the deck of the old bar

p-town sign: remember
sharks hunt seals
seals outswim sharks
people don't!

sunset
provincetown seagull
dips into
the blue

race point beach
cranberries
scrub pines
smell of hawaiian tropic
coconut oil

dog walkers
man filming birds
one bright orange towel
left in the dunes

bare feet
hot sand
collecting shells
red stones
turquoise sea

i'm gonna stroke this day
onto watercolor paper
and take it back to
syracuse, ny

nodding off
to basho
beach campfire almost out

kites on the beach
children flying
rainbows

Janine

commercial street
cat lying next to buddha statue
in zen bookstore window
i pay nothing

a judy drag queen
passes me on the beach
last munchkin is dead

pink blue indigo
boats bopping on the ocean
july sunset

mapplethorpe
flowers
dicks
and patty smith
while old cape cod
plays
in an antique store
on commercial street

balthus
loved
his cats &
prepubescent girls
i love sax
& biking through
the dunes
of the cape—

that's life

used bookstore
in provincetown
a black cat
dreaming
beside a first edition
of
apollinaire

coming into town
a row of little white and green cottages
i know i am almost there

guess where
a seagull
on mcmillan's
wharf
a sunset on
herring cove
sea grass moving
in the wind
guitar player
in the square
kid eating ice cream
drag queen
rollerblading by

my book of poems
arrived 2 days ago
the sea is calm

the ocean
eats a fat woman
like a slice of pizza

humpback whales
lunge their huge
renoir women
bodies above the sea

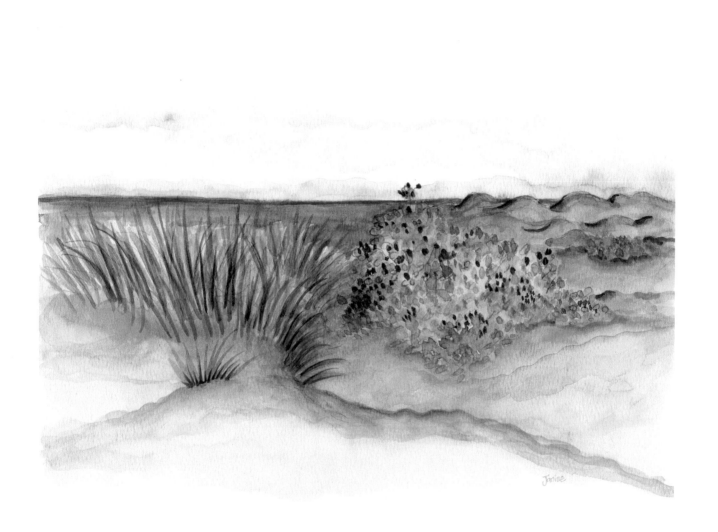

109

Printed in the United States
By Bookmasters